Patti Beth

Forgiveness and Implicit Theories in Early Adolescents

Patti Beth

Forgiveness and Implicit Theories in Early Adolescents

VDM Verlag Dr. Müller

Imprint

Bibliographic information by the German National Library: The German National Library lists this publication at the German National Bibliography; detailed bibliographic information is available on the Internet at http://dnb.d-nb.de.

Any brand names and product names mentioned in this book are subject to trademark, brand or patent protection and are trademarks or registered trademarks of their respective holders. The use of brand names, product names, common names, trade names, product descriptions etc. even without a particular marking in this works is in no way to be construed to mean that such names may be regarded as unrestricted in respect of trademark and brand protection legislation and could thus be used by anyone.

Cover image: www.purestockx.com

Publisher:
VDM Verlag Dr. Müller Aktiengesellschaft & Co. KG, Dudweiler Landstr. 125 a, 66123 Saarbrücken, Germany,
Phone +49 681 9100-698, Fax +49 681 9100-988,
Email: info@vdm-verlag.de

Produced in USA and UK by:
Lightning Source Inc., La Vergne, Tennessee, USA
Lightning Source UK Ltd., Milton Keynes, UK
BookSurge LLC, 5341 Dorchester Road, Suite 16, North Charleston, SC 29418, USA

ISBN: 978-3-8364-7492-4

Table of Contents

List of Tables

List of Figures

Forgiveness and Implicit Theories in Early Adolescents

Patti Beth, Ph.D.

University of Wisconsin-Madison

The purpose of this study was to test implicit theory change as a way to help young adolescents forgive a peer who hurt them deeply. Participants were 163 fourth, fifth, and sixth grade children aged 9(57), 10(56), and 11(48) with 2 withdrawn. Participants were recruited from community elementary and middle schools in a medium-sized Midwestern city and from area YMCA summer day camps. Implicit theories were assessed by the Implicit Theory Questionnaire (Erdley & Dweck, 1993), and levels of forgiveness and expectations to be hurt again were measured by the Enright Forgiveness Inventory for Children (EFI-C; Enright, 1993) and the Offense Expectation Scale for Children and Adolescents (Beth) in Study 1. Results showed that those holding an *incremental* theory of attribution are more forgiving than those holding an *entity* view. Overall feelings of vulnerability to future hurt were higher for entity theorists. Being thought of as weak was a major concern to all of the children in this study.

Study 2 measured the impact an intervention designed to change one's implicit theory from entity toward an incremental view would have on levels of forgiveness, expectations of future hurt, and levels of anger measure by the Beck Anger Inventory for Youth (BANI-Y). Participants were 54 of the 163 from Study 1 who subscribed to an entity theory, randomly assigned to an experimental (n = 27) and a control group (n = 27). It was expected that young adolescents would become more forgiving and less worried about future hurt as their implicit theories changed. Analysis of variance revealed a significant interaction between the experimental and control groups in favor of the intervention, demonstrated by an increase in forgiveness for the experimental group at the immediate post-test and at the follow-up post-test, and a decrease in the concern for future hurt at the follow-up post test.

Chapter 1: Introduction

This research was conducted to examine how the attributions for behavior that young adolescents make are related to their willingness to forgive a peer who has hurt them deeply. Being hurt by a peer typically involves being repeatedly criticized, ridiculed, or bullied. Peer rejection can include social withdrawal, social anxiety, depression, and feelings of hostility and revenge. Research conducted under the supervision of Dr. Enright demonstrates that forgiveness instruction to angry adolescents increases forgiveness, improves attitudes toward school and teachers, betters relationships with parents and peers, and even improves grades (Gambaro, 2002). The hope of these studies is to provide further development of teacher and parent led interventions that will foster forgiveness and reduce the negative thoughts and feelings inherent in anger, thereby reducing the expression of anger (Enright & Fitzgibbons, 2000). It may be that believing others' behavior is attributed to enduring traits, such as badness, induces feelings of hatred fueled by the fear of being hurt again.

The work of Robert D. Enright and his colleagues has demonstrated that forgiveness can reduce anger and increase emotional health (Enright & Fitzgibbons, 2000). The primary goal of this study was to explore those psychological variables that will help children and adolescents to forgive one another when wronged, rather than to seek revenge. When an individual is offended, the pain induces feelings of revenge that can be dissuaded by psychological dimensions comprising the act of forgiveness (Enright & Fitzgibbons, 2000). These psychological dimensions are framed and strongly influenced by our own personal implicit theories of how the world works (Dweck, Chiu, & Hong1995). If ways to aid children and adolescents to forgive can be found, it is hoped that anger may also be reduced, and subsequently school aggression and violence.

Enright and his colleagues (Enright & the Human Development Study Group, 1994) found that ability to consider the context in which the offending behavior occurred is one of the first steps in a process of change that leads to the development of forgiveness. The aim is not to condone the offending behavior, but to consider the contextual factors that influenced it's occurrence. By reframing the event and thus considering the pressures the offender was under, one can step closer to experiencing empathy for the offender. Enright and North (1998) state that reframing is not only a way of putting the wrongdoer and his action in context, but is also a way of psychologically separating the wrongdoer from the crime that has been committed. It is this separation that allows for an understanding of unconditional worth. To reframe is to rethink a situation and to see it with a new perspective. Considering contextual factors helps the individual to accept that the offender is a human being who possesses worth regardless of his or her behavior. This acceptance allows for the development of empathy and compassion toward the offender. However, if a person feels unsafe around the offender it will be difficult "to step inside their shoes," if only hypothetically.

Some people hold an implicit theory that defines the offender as a "bad person," believing that hurting behavior is indicative of the offender's entire personality (Chiu, Hong, & Dweck, 1997). They understand behavior to be the result of stable and enduring personality traits. Because of this belief, individuals holding this type of implicit theory may find forgiving more difficult because of a fear they will be hurt again. It is reasoned that the "bad person" cannot help but behave badly. In contrast, if one who has been deeply hurt is helped to consider that contextual factors were largely responsible for the other's behavior, they will be better enabled to understand that the offender is not necessarily predisposed to hurt them again. The behavior occurred not because the offender is a bad person, but because of circumstances surrounding the event. There is some evidence of individual differences in the pattern and time spent working through the process of forgiveness (Park, 1989). These differences may be due to individual differences in implicit theories.

The notion that people form implicit theories about their world that can influence their social understanding has been introduced, researched, and discussed by both social psychologists as early as Heider (1958) and Kelly (1967), and in the not too distant past by developmental psychologists such as Wellman (1990), Gelman (Gelman, Coley, & Gottfried, 1994, for review), and more recently by Dweck and her colleagues (Dweck & Ehrlinger, 2005). Dweck has examined how specific theories are related to various dimensions of social attribution. A key finding by Dweck is that around the ages of 7 or 8, some children develop different patterns of social judgment (Erdley & Dweck, 1993). These patterns reflect individual differences in implicit theories. If someone possesses an entity, or fixed theory, he or she thinks that behavior is linked to stable or fixed and enduring personality traits. If someone subscribes to an incremental theory, he or she believes that behavior can be best explained by the situation in which it occurs, as well as other less salient contextual factors.

Entity theorists believe behaviors they have once observed are diagnostic of certain personality traits, even when they may see current evidence to the contrary (Levy & Dweck, 1998). This holds true for both their own and others' behavior. Entity theorists not only predict more stability of behaviors over time, but typically recommend greater punishment for negative behavior (Levy & Dweck, 1998). In contrast, incremental theorists are more likely to be flexible in their judgments, generally taking situational or contextual information into account. They do not predict stable behavior over time, and feel more empathy for the offender than do entity theorists.

The belief that one's worth is not defined by his or her behavior, (be it positive or negative), reflects a major difference in belief systems between an entity theorist and an incremental theorist (Heyman and Dweck, 1998). An entity theorist tends to regard others (and themselves) as one and the same with their behavior. They see personality traits and characteristics as explanations and predictions for behavior. In contrast, an incremental theorist sees behavior as being determined by situational or contextual factors. They consider such factors to be situational pressures that the offending person was under at the time. In addition, incrementalists consider what they may know about the offender's developmental history.

It is the thesis of this study that children and adolescents who hold an incremental implicit theory will find it easier to forgive. This is, in part, because incremental theorists look to the situation to explain behavior enabling them to be free to feel empathy for the offender, and; in part, because they do not necessarily expect to be hurt again by the offender. It is the primary purpose of this study to examine the utility of teaching early adolescents to forgive, rather than to seek revenge, by helping them to consider contextual factors surrounding a deep hurt. There is ample evidence showing that when implicit theories are temporarily induced, individuals show similar social judgment patterns to those of individuals with pre-existing theories (Levy & Dweck, 1998).

Forgiveness

Dr. Robert Enright's research has shown that people who forgive can decrease anger, anxiety, and depression (Enright & Fitzgibbons, 2000). Studies conducted by Enright and his colleagues demonstrate that forgiveness is linked to healthy emotional regulation (Baskin & Enright, 2005; Lin, Mach, Enright, Baskin, & Krahn, 2005). Forgiveness has a specific task: to help people overcome resentment, bitterness, and even hatred toward others who have treated them unfairly and at times cruelly. This task is accomplished through a process that involves cognitive, emotional, and behavioral change. Forgiveness is a developmental and qualitative variable that shifts perspectives, feelings, attitudes, behaviors, and interactions. This shift denotes moving in a new direction: from judgmental to understanding, from resentful to loving, from anxious to relaxed, and from conflicted to cooperative. Enright (Enright & Fitzgibbons, 2000) states that the philosopher Joanna North's definition of forgiveness provides the best foundation for his process model of forgiveness. Following North's (1987) ideas, forgiveness is defined as follows:

People upon rationally determining that they have been unfairly treated, forgive when they willfully abandon resentment and related responses (to which they have a right), and endeavor to respond to the wrongdoer based on the moral principle of beneficence, which may include compassion, unconditional worth, generosity, and moral love (to which the wrongdoer, by nature of the hurtful act or acts, has no right).

Forgiveness research demonstrates that forgiveness intervention programs can be effective. Hebl and Enright (1993) published the first ever empirically based intervention on forgiveness. The process model was tested with 24 elderly women (M = 74.5 years). Two patterns emerged, one dealing with the degree of forgiveness offered to a specific offender and the other with a general tendency to consider forgiveness when injustices arise. Al-Mabuk, Enright, and Cardis (1995) reported two studies done with late adolescents who experienced neglect growing up. After the forgiveness intervention, the experimental group improved in two dimensions of forgiveness, in trait anxiety, self-esteem, and in hope and attitude toward their parents. Freedman and Enright (1996) tested the model with 12 female incest survivors. Beyond statistical gains, participants reported feeling good about their experience in forgiving their perpetrator. Most felt that forgiving the sexual abuser helped in areas other than the incest, such as with their own families now and at work. Coyle and Enright (1997) tested a forgiveness intervention with 10 men who reported that they were emotionally hurt by the abortion decision of their partner. These men suffered a higher anxiety mean score (M = 57) at pretest than did the women who were incest survivors (M = 50). After the intervention program, their anxiety dropped from an average of 57.66 (above published norms) to 38.33 (normal levels). The men also showed as much as an 86 point improvement on the Enright Forgiveness Inventory (Lin, Mach, Enright, Baskin, & Krahn, 2005; EFI, Subkoviak et al., 1992, 1995).

Anger

A key objective of forgiveness therapy, or invention, involves helping an individual who has been deeply hurt to reduce their feelings of anger. Anger includes strong negative thoughts and feelings, and can be expressed both verbally and behaviorally. When someone is angry, he or she experiences physiological arousal and the related emotional pain to unfair treatment or frustration. The following seven points illustrate anger characterized as the center of forgiveness therapy by Enright and Fitzgibbons (2000):

1) The anger is focused on another person or other people.

2) The anger is intense, at least in the short term.

3) The anger often leads to a learned pattern of annoyance, irritation, and acrimony with others who may or may not be the source of the anger.

4) The anger can be extreme in its passivity or its overt hostility.

5) The anger is sometimes regressive, appropriate for those much younger.

6) The anger abides.

7) The anger is based on a real injustice and hurt, not some fanciful occurrence irrationally perceived.

In regards to children and adolescents, anger can result from hurt and disappointment with parents and siblings, and/or hurt and rejection by peers. Peer rejection typically involves being repeatedly criticized, ridiculed, or bullied by others. Symptoms of peer rejection include social withdrawal, social anxiety, depression, and unfortunately, hostile treatment of others. Research conducted under the supervision of Dr. Enright demonstrates that forgiveness instruction to angry adolescents increases forgiveness, improves attitudes toward school and teachers, betters relationships with parents and peers, and even improves grades (Gambaro, 2002). This research was conducted in order to provide further development of teacher and parent led interventions that will foster forgiveness and reduce the negative thoughts and feelings inherent in anger, thereby reducing the expression of anger (Enright & Fitzgibbons, 2000). It may be that believing others' behavior is attributed to enduring traits, such as badness, induces feelings of hatred fueled by fear, the fear of being hurt over and over again.

Forgiveness in Children and Adolescents

The excessive expression of anger in children and teenagers in the U.S. has increased since the 1980s. A Uniform Crime Report from the late 90s showed an increase in the arrests of children and teens under age 18 in such areas as aggravated assault, murder, non-negligent manslaughter, and burglary (Federal Bureau of Investigation, 1998). Depression, suicide rates, CD, and substance abuse among adolescents have increased (Fombonne, 1998). Fombonne (1998) found that the rates of suicide and substance abuse in adolescents almost doubled between 1979 and 1990. Aggressive behavior patterns are the most common reason for referral among psychiatrically referred children and adolescents. The number of juveniles arrested for violent crimes increased 64% between 1987 and 1994 (Snyder, 1994). More recently, serious violent crime involving juvenile victims and offenders went up between 2002 and 2003. In 2003, 18 per 1,000 juveniles were victims of serious violent crimes, that is, homicide, rape, aggravated assault, and robbery, and 15 per 1,000 juveniles were reported by victims to have committed such crimes. These rates increased from those in 2002, when 10 per 1,000 youth were victims of serious crimes and 11 per 1,000 juveniles were identified as offenders. Undeniably, there is an urgent need to help youths find a positive functional solution to the anger they feel.

Unfortunately, one of the ways children and adolescents cope with anger by expressing it. This expression can be open and direct, or carried out in a passive-aggressive manner. Expressed anger is often excessive and misdirected. Several past studies report that 21% of middle school children (Boulton & Underwood, 1992) and 22% in elementary school (Austin & Joseph, 1996) have been bullied. Their peers regularly side with the bullies against them and even develop their own feelings of anger toward them. As a result of this harsh and unfair treatment by their peers, these children and adolescents may develop regularly intense anger and even violent impulses for revenge against their tormentors. Teachers report not being confident in their ability to deal with bullying, and 87% want more training (Boulton, 1997). Bullying

and being victimized by bullies have been recognized recently as health problems for school

children because of their association with a range of adjustment problems, including poor mental

health and violent behavior. Larger and more recent studies suggest that 20% to 30% of students

are frequently involved in bullying as perpetrators and/or victims (Juvonen, Graham, & Schuster,

2003). http://pediatrics.aappublications.org/cgi/content/full/112/6/1231 - R2#R2 More than one

in five 12-year-olds are repeatedly either bullies, victims or both, and bullies are often popular

and viewed by classmates as the "coolest" in their classes, according to new research from the

most comprehensive study on young adolescent bullying in an ethnically diverse, large urban

setting (Rand, 2005). There is an immediate need to develop programs that educators can use to

help children and adolescents resolve their anger and impulses for revenge, rather than to act

violently upon their hurt.

The experience of anger can lead to a desire for revenge, which may not diminish until

the existence of the resentful feelings is uncovered and subsequently resolved. Without

resolution, anger can be displaced for many years onto others and erupt decades later in loving

relationships. Anger may not be fully resolved until a conscious decision is made to work on

forgiving the offender. During childhood, another of the most common methods of coping with

anger is denial (Boulton, 1997). However, there are serious dangers attached to this form of

coping with the anger. Denial can cause emotional and psychological harm, as well as increase

feelings of sadness, guilt and shame, and the misdirection of anger and resentment toward others.

To date, research has offered little to the clinical literature on the use of forgiveness with

children and adolescents (Fitzgibbons, 1986; 1998; Park, 1989; Hope, 1987). In general,

children neither understand, nor know how to deal with their angry feelings and impulses for revenge. Typically, they are aware of only two ways to deal with their anger, to deny it or express it. Few young people understand that there is a third option available to them, understanding and forgiving those who hurt them. When appropriately taught, forgiveness can resolve strong feelings of anger in children and adolescents, including violent impulses, and assist in the clinical treatment of many child and adolescent disorders (Enright & Fitzgibons, 2000).

Many children and adolescents (as well as adults) have misconceptions about what forgiveness is. Considering these misconceptions, it becomes important to teach children what forgiveness is not. Specifically, forgiveness is not tolerating and enabling angry, abusive people to express their anger toward you. Forgiveness does not mean being a doormat or acting in a weak manner. Forgiveness should not limit healthy assertiveness. Importantly, one does not have to trust or reconcile with those who are abusive, insensitive, or show no motivation to change their unacceptable behavior. Forgiving someone does not necessarily mean going to that person and telling them that you have forgiven them. Children may fear that forgiving makes them appear weak, sanctioning the hurt they have felt, and that they will be hurt again if they tell the perpetrator about their willingness to forgive. This fear may be magnified if one feels that someone who hurt them is a bad person (entity theorist), therefore being constrained by this badness to hurt them again.

The understanding that an individual possesses unconditional worth plays a key role in the forgiveness process (Lin, Mach, Enright, Baskin, & Krahn, 2005; Enright & the Human Development Study Group,1991). Unconditional worth requires the insight that the offender is a person. The forgiver sees that no matter what another does, he or she is still of worth, worthy of respect because of personhood. Even if the other hurts me deeply, we are equal in that we are both human beings. In other words, the offense is not a defining characteristic of one who did wrong (on unconditional worth and respect for an offender, see Enright & the Human Development Study Group, 1994; Holmgren, 1993, 1997). That one's worth is not defined by their behavior (be it positive or negative) is a major belief difference between an entity theorist and an incremental theorist. An entity theorist tends to regard others (and themselves) as one and the same with their behavior. They see personality traits and characteristics as explanations and predictions for behavior. In contrast, an incremental theorist sees behavior as being determined by situational or contextual factors. They consider such factors as the pressures that the offending person was under at the time, as well as what they may know about the offender's history. During the process of forgiveness, reframing a hurtful event by learning to view the wrongdoer in context, allows one to feel empathy for the offender. This step in forgiveness will be easier, and perhaps quicker, for the incremental theorist because he or she is accustomed to looking to the situation or context for causal explanations.

Enright and Fitzgibbons (2000, p. 63) state that: "The inability to forgive or disinterest in forgiving often is the result of the client paying much more attention to the other's behaviors than anything else. In many cases, the client is concentrating on the offender's specific behaviors of offense and defining the offender exclusively in those terms." A forgiveness intervention is needed that focuses on reframing behavior by the context surrounding it. This will allow the individual to separate the offense from the offender, enable feelings of empathy, and abandon resentment.

Implicit Theories in Children and Adolescents

During the 1980s, studies on young children's understanding of the psychological causes of behavior led researchers to conclude, because there was a developmental shift in the use of causal attributions from external, situationally based attributions by younger children to internal, trait-based attributions by older school-aged children, this shift was part of the natural course of development (Shantz, et al., 1983; Flavell, 1985). This conclusion found support in the person-perception literature (Barenboim, 1981; Secord & Peevers, 1974), with studies showing that children do not consistently understand traits to be stable dispositions before 7- or 8- years of age. This is also the age at which children show a dramatic shift in their use of personality trait terms in their descriptions of others (Barenboim, 1981; Livesley & Bromly. 1973). In these studies, children prior to the age of 7 tended to describe others in terms of contextual qualities such as appearance, possessions, and place of residence. Recent studies in the United States have again found the greatest shift toward trait explanations occurs around age 7- or 8- years old (Yuill, 1998; Heyman and Dweck, 1998).

Although children around 7- or 8 years-old understand that traits can be defined as stable and enduring qualities, Dweck and her colleagues (Dweck, Chiu, & Hong, 1995) found some children continue to look to the situation for explanations of their own and others' behavior. Initially, Dweck's work centered on the academic achievement domain and found children who believe their intelligence to be fixed focus on evaluating and measuring their own intelligence by academic failure. In contrast, those who believe intelligence is a malleable trait focus on developing their ability. Later studies examined the influences implicit theories produce in the social domains.

Erdley, Dweck, Loomis, Cain, and Dumas-Hines, (1997) found a relationship between children's goals in social situations and their responses to social failure, and that these goals are predicted by children's theories about their personality. Entity theorists were more focused on performance goals (seeking to gain positive judgments of themselves and avoid negative evaluations) than were incremental theorists who focused more on learning new strategies for overcoming rejection. Moreover, children who enter a challenging social situation with a focus on performance goals were more likely to react to failure helplessly and defensively. Heyman and Dweck (1998) found that 7- and 8-year-old children, who could be classified as entity theorists, viewed sociomoral behavior as being more closely linked to stable traits than did incremental theorists. They were more likely to conclude that a new child in class who lies to gain the approval of other children is a "bad kid" (73% entity vs. 23.3% incremental). Entity theorists were more likely to report expectations of cross-situational generality (88.5% vs. 46.7%). They were also more likely to agree with a positive sociomoral stability item, stating that a child who behaved in a friendly manner would always be friendly (84.6% vs. 50% incremental).

Levy & Dweck (1999) recently examined how differences in implicit theories might impact understanding, judging, and reacting to groups and their members. Young adolescents were told about several negative and neutral behaviors performed by different students in an unknown school. Those holding entity theories more strongly associated negative attributes with the entire school, judging them more extremely on negative traits and perceiving group members to be more similar on negative traits than incremental theorists did (entity theorists: $M = -2.43$, incremental theorists: $M = -1.46$). Entity theorists expected an unknown student from the negative school (not included in the stories they heard) to be relatively mean and bad, however, the incremental theorists' ratings of the unknown student indicated that their expectation was a neutral one ($M = -0.03$). Entity theorists relied heavily on trait explanations. The amount of interaction they wished to have with the group's members also differed. Entity theorists more frequently reported that they did not want to socialize with students from the unknown school. Studies have found many striking belief differences between the two theory types (Chiu, Hong, & Dweck,1997; Erdley & Dweck, 1993; Hong, 1994; Levy & Dweck, 1998b; Levy et al., 1998; Plaks & Dweck, 1997; Sorich & Dweck, 1996; Chiu, 1994).

Similar patterns of attribution have been studied concerning blame, and how these attributions affect people in various contexts. Attributions can be either external (i.e., blaming the situation), or internal (i.e., blaming oneself or others). One such context studied how attributions affected the way in which children cope with injury. Gable and Peterson (1998) found that when children attributed their injuries to external causes, they reported less post-injury fear, pain, and distress. In contrast, internally focused attributions, such as self-blame, often result in negative psychological sequelae (Abramson, Seligman, & Teasdale, 1978; Seligman, 1975).

Cognitive errors involving self-blame have been implicated in playing a role in the development of depressive symptoms in children (Nolen-Hoeksena, Girgus, & Segilman, 1992). In a recent study of children's appraisal of major life events, Hasan and Power (2004) found that faulty outcome and duration expectancies, such as believing that negative consequences are stable and long-lasting, contribute to psychopathology in children in that they involve catastrophizing the outcomes of ambiguous events. When children continually tend to overestimate the danger of potentially stressful situations, anxiety disorders begin to develop (Bogels & Zigterman, 2000). Inward-focused negative emotions, such as self-blame and guilt, are activated when individuals hold themselves responsible for negative outcomes. However, in the context of injustice perceptions, blaming the other party is associated with negative outward emotions such as anger and hostility (Tangney & Dearing, 2002). These attributions occur when individuals experience a personal slight, demeaning offense, or harmful action (Lazarus, 1991). All of these negative beliefs, written about in the literature on blame, are indicative of an entity theory. Considering the possible pathological outcomes of such cognitive errors, training in implicit theory and positive change toward an incremental view may be warranted.

Although implicit theories can be relatively stable, they can be changed through intervention. In recent intervention studies, various strategies to teach incremental theories have been quite successful. In a management setting, Heslin, Lathan, and VandeWalle (2005) taught managers an incremental theory by means of an article, film, and self-persuasion exercises. After training, the managers were significantly more helpful with and sensitive to improvement in their employees' performance than was a control group. This openness to positive change in others is important for conflict resolution. Changing people's theories about themselves also can lead to more effective conflict resolution. In the Nussaum and Dweck (2005) studies, teaching an incremental theory made participants more willing to admit and address their flaws and less likely to look for flaws in others. Blackwell, Trzesniewski, and Dweck (2005) conducted an intervention to teach adolescents an incremental theory of intelligence. After the intervention, teachers reported an upsurge in the desire to learn and willingness to invest effort by students who had previously been apathetic and defensive. Two other studies have replicated these results with junior high school students and with college students (Good, Aronson, & Inzlicht, 2003; Aronson, Fried, & Good, 2002). As previously mentioned, Levy and colleagues (Levy & Dweck, 1999: Levy, Stroessner, & Dweck, 1998) demonstrated that entity theorist were more prone to forming stereotypes, to seeing groups as overly homogeneous, and to seeing negatively stereotyped groups as completely distinct from themselves. These studies also demonstrated that these tendencies could be reversed by reading a scientific article supporting an incremental view to the participants. In sum, recent studies have shown that changing people's implicit theories, by teaching them an incremental view, results in a reduction in the tendency to label and stereotype, an increase in sensitivity to progress and change, and an upswing in their desire to learn, all important qualities for resolving differences and for openness to forgiveness.

In sum (Levy, Stroessner, & Dweck, 1998),

Entity theorists believe:

1) People's qualities are fixed over time and across situations.

2) Traits are the primary causes of behavior.

3) Traits are the building blocks of personality and refer to deep-seated qualities.

4) People's traits are reliably expressed in behavior; therefore, traits are easy to judge.

5) Members of groups share traits; there is little within-group variability with respect to traits.

Incremental theorists believe:

1) People's qualities are changeable over time and across situations.

2) Context-sensitive psychological variables are the primary causes of behavior.

3) Traits refer to summaries of behavior rather to a person's underlying character.

4) Because of dynamic factors, it is difficult to make judgments based on scant information.

5) Members of a group may not be similar to one another, for example, because of environmental factors.

Chapter 2: The Current Studies

It was the thesis of these studies that early adolescents who hold an incremental implicit theory are more forgiving. This is, in part, because incremental theorists will find it easier to experience empathy for the offender due to their causal beliefs regarding the offense (framed in context provides for the understanding of unconditional worth). And in part, incremental theorists do not uniformly expect to be hurt again by the offender because they regard behavior to be causally linked to the context in which it occurs, and not to negative traits (bad person).

It was the primary purpose of the proposed studies to examine the utility of teaching early adolescents to forgive, rather than to seek revenge, by considering contextual factors such as the situation in which the hurtful behavior occurred. For example, Dweck (Dweck & Leggett, 1988) experimentally manipulated children's theories of intelligence by presenting a passage that portrayed the intelligence of notable individuals (e.g., Albert Einstein) as either fixed or malleable. The results showed the induction affected children's goal choice on an upcoming task: Children in the entity condition showed greater concern with how intelligence would be judged, whereas, children in the incremental condition showed greater concern with developing their ability. Other studies with late adolescents have shown that when theories about the malleability of traits are temporarily induced, individuals show similar patterns to those of individuals with pre-existing incremental theories (Levy & Dweck, 1998).

Generally, it was expected that the scores of young adolescents who can be classified as entity theorists on the Implicit Personality Theory Questionnaire (Erdley and Dweck, 1993) will reflect a shift toward the incremental theory view after a reframing intervention focused on context-related causal explanations for an offense. It was also expected that the entity theorists' scores on the Enright Forgiveness Inventory for Children (EFI -C; Enright, 1993) will show an increased propensity to forgive others after the reframing intervention, and that their feelings

of anger will diminish. Several related hypotheses were tested in Study 1 and Study 2.

They are specifically as follows:

Study 1:

1) It was expected that those holding an incremental theory would be more forgiving than

those who hold an entity theory.

2) It was expected that those holding an entity theory would have higher overall expectations for

future hurt than incremental theorists.

3) It was expected that those holding an entity theory will have higher expectations for future

hurt from the specific person who hurt them deeply, than incremental theorists.

4) Feelings of vulnerability would be higher for entity theorists than for incremental theorists if

they are asked to forgive an individual who hurt them deeply. It was expected that these feelings

are because of negative personality traits attributed to the offender.

Study 2:

1) It was expected that after context-related causal explanation training, the scores of those

holding an entity theory would reflect an increase in forgiveness and a decrease in expectations

to be hurt again at both immediate and follow-up post-tests.

2) The greatest increase in forgiveness was expected to be found immediately after the training

was completed. Some diminution was expected because of only one training presentation. The

development of a knowledge base in any domain plays a vital role in memory performance

(Rogoff & Mistry, 1990).

3) It was also expected that the greatest decrease in expectations to be hurt again would be found immediately after training.

4) It was expected that there will be a positive relationship between the scores on the Implicit Personality Theory Questionnaire (reflecting a shift toward an incremental theory) and the scores on the EFI-C (most forgiving).

5) It was expected that those showing the least shift in perspective toward an incremental view would also feel the most vulnerable to future hurt from one who has deeply hurt them in the past if they are asked to forgive that individual. Therefore, there would be a negative relationship between the scores from the Implicit Personality Theory Questionnaire and the scores from the Specific/Conditional sub-scale of the OES-AC designed to measure expectations of future hurt from someone who has hurt one deeply if one were to forgive that individual (see Method section for full description of the OES-AC).

6) It was expected that entity theorists in the experimental condition would show a greater reduction in general feelings of anger than entity theorists in the control condition, after the context-related causal explanation training.

Chapter 3: Method - Study 1

Participants

The total number of participants was 163 fourth, fifth, and sixth grade children. The

average age was 9.94 years. (57were 9 year-olds, 56 were 10 year-olds, 48 were 11 year-olds, 2

withdrawn) Participants were recruited from various community elementary and middle schools

in a medium-sized Midwestern city and from area YMCA summer day camps. There was an

overall 20% response rate. Information regarding gender, racial, and ethnic background was not

collected because these factors have not demonstrated any links to differences in implicit

theories in past studies (Erdley & Dweck, 1993). Informed consent letters were required to be

signed by the children's parent or legal guardian before they were allowed to participate, and 11-

year-olds were also required to sign informed consent letters in accordance with human subjects

requirements. The Implicit Personality Questionnaire (Erdley & Dweck, 1993),used in this

study, generally yields a middle group, as high as one-third of the children tested, that cannot be

clearly classified as either incremental or entity theorists. Participants were classified according

to their scores on the Implicit Personality Theory Questionnaire (scores can range from 1 to 6,

strongly agree to strongly disagree) using the cut off scores established by the validation studies

of Erdley and Dweck (1993, see Measurements section). A score of 2.33 or less resulted in a

classification of entity theorist, and a score of 3.67 or greater resulted in a classification of

incremental theorist. Those children whose scores fell between 2.33 and 3.67 were classified as

Mid. These classifications resulted in 54 entity theorists, 75 incremental theorists, and 32 whose

score fell in the Mid-range classification. Two participants did not complete the study because

they reported they that had not experienced a deep hurt from a peer in the within the last year.

The Enright Forgiveness Inventory for Children (EFI-C; Enright, 1993) first asks the child to remember a time when a peer "hurt you very, very much." If a child could not recall a

qualifying event defined as a deep hurt from a peer within the last year, they could not continue

as a participant. It was explained to each child that a peer was defined as a friend, neighbor,

someone at your place of worship or a club that you are in, who is around your own age and that

you see on a regular basis, but not a family member.

Measurements

The Implicit Personality Theory Questionnaire

The Implicit Personality Theory Questionnaire was designed by Erdley and Dweck,

(1993) to assess individual differences in children's beliefs about the nature of people's

personalities. This measure asks the children to indicate on a scale from 1 (really agree) to 6

(really disagree), the extent to which they believe each of these three statements:

a) Someone's personality is something about them that they can't change very much.

b) A person can do things to get people to like them, but they can't change their personality.

c) Everyone has a certain personality, and it is something that they can't do much about.

Erdley & Dweck (1993) choose a small number of questions for the purposes of tapping a

very specific belief system. Items chosen for use in the scale were those that had the highest

correlations with other items from a previously tested larger sample. Test-retest reliability over a

one week period was .64 (p < .01). During initial validity studies, two distinct groups of children

were typically formed after completing the Implicit Personality Scale (Erdley & Dweck, 1993).

For example, from a group of 135 children, 53 could be classified as entity theorists (range = 1.00 - 2.33), and 40 children could be classified as incremental theorists (n = 40, range = 3.67 - 6.00). To increase the robustness of the results, those whose scores fell between 2.33 and 3.67 were omitted from further analysis (n = 42). Erdley and Dweck, (1993) state that only the fixed or entity choice is presented because previous pilot studies show when both options are presented, children tended to favor incremental statements, and this tendency increased as they worked through a series of statements.

The Likert scale format, originally used by Erdley and Dweck (1993), is preferred for the present study. Although Dweck (Heyman & Dweck 1998) later tested a forced answer format that allowed for the classification of all children, robustness of the results were significantly reduced. In part II of their 1993 study (Erdley and Dweck, 1993), Dweck experimented with the implicit personality scale by adding a fourth question: d) A person can change the way they act, but they can't change their real personality. However, this did little or nothing to alter the group classifications. The present author believes this fourth question may also blur any distinctions between behavior and personality in such a way as to add confusion to a previously chosen implicit theory, and it's subsequent relation to forgiveness. Therefore, the originally designed and tested Implicit Personality Questionnaire (Erdley & Dweck, 1993) will be used for the proposed study.

The Enright Forgiveness Inventory for Children

The Enright Forgiveness Inventory for Children (EFI-C; Enright, 1993) is adapted from the from the Enright Forgiveness Scale designed for use with late adolescents and adults (EFI; Subkoviak, Enright, Wu, Gassin, Freedman, Olson, Sarinopoulos, 1992; Subkoviak, Enright, Wu, Gassin, Freedman, Olson, Sarinopoulos, 1995). When a person forgives, he or she offers a degree of positive affect (how one feels about the offender), cognition (how one thinks about the offender), and behavior (how one acts toward the offending person), and to some degree should demonstrate the absence of negative affect, cognition, and behavior. A valid measure of forgiveness must also rule out false responses or pseudo-forgiveness, such as condoning, excusing, or denying what happened.

The Enright Forgiveness Inventory for Children (EFI-C; Enright, 1993) is a 30-item interview designed for use by a researcher or clinician to assess a child or adolescent's feelings regarding an event in which they were deeply hurt. In this study the event was strictly limited to a deep hurt from a peer. Forgiveness operates in the context of a personal injustice that the respondent has experienced (Subkoviak et al.; 1992, 1995). Therefore, the child is first asked to remember a time when a peer "hurt you very, very much." This instrument is designed, after a series of questions contained in the interview to allow for the experimenter to determine if the event described requires forgiveness. In cases such as this, the child would be asked for a different event and the interview would begin again. However, in these studies, all the events described by the participants were deep hurts. Therefore, it was not necessary to probe further for qualifying events.

Of the test questions, 10 involve current affect (5 positive e.g., friendly, 5 negative e.g., mad), 10 involve current thoughts, or cognition, about the person (5 positive e.g., good thoughts, 5 negative e.g., a bad person), and 10 target intended behavior (5 positive e.g., helping, 5 negative e.g., getting back at him/her). A 4-point Likert format page is used to record participants responses from a response board. The EFI-C generates a total forgiveness score as well as scores on six sub-scales: positive and negative affect, positive and negative cognition, and positive and negative behavior. The range on each item is from 1 to 4 (yes, a little bit yes, a little bit no, no) and the total score ranges from 30 (most unforgiving) to 120 (most forgiving). Previous research reported that the alpha coefficient of the EFI-C was .94 (Park, 1989), and more recent studies in Belfast, Northern Ireland report a Chronbach's alpha of .91 (Hepp-Dax, 1996; Gambaro, 2002; Enright & Ludwikoski, 2003). Validity of the measure is supported by the forgiveness intervention conducted in Belfast that showed significant reductions in children's anger when compared to a control group who did not receive the intervention (Enright & Ludwikoski, 2003). As forgiveness scores on the EFI-C rose, anger scores measured by Beck's Anger Inventory for Youth (BANI-Y) dropped.

The Offense Expectation Scale for Children and Adolescents

For purposes of the proposed study, a scale was developed to assess the participants' beliefs about the likelihood of being deeply hurt again in the future. It was hypothesized that incremental theorists do not uniformly expect to be hurt again by the offender because they regard behavior to be causally linked to the context in which it occurs, and not to negative traits (bad person). The opposite would be true for entity theorists. A scale was needed to measure expectations for future hurt and if these expectations were conditioned upon forgiveness. As stated previously, when a person forgives, he or she offers a degree of positive affect (how one feels about the offender), cognition (how one thinks about the offender), and behavior (how one acts toward the offending person), and to some degree should demonstrate the absence of negative affect, cognition, and behavior. Therefore, a scale to measure the expectation of future hurt, and whether or not this expectation is conditioned upon forgiving, should also address affect, cognition, and behavior. The Offense Expectation Scale for Children and Adolescents (OES- CA; Beth) is designed to assess beliefs, feelings, and behavioral attitudes concerning the offender who served as the subject for the EFI-C interview, as well as generalized beliefs about being hurt again. Generalized beliefs about vulnerability were important to learning if fears of future hurt were strictly related to the offender or reflected a more generalized concern. To begin, the child was asked to think about the person who hurt them deeply. Instructions were given to each participant as follows:

"These questions may sound very similar, but some deal with thoughts, some with worries and feelings, and some with how you might act, so please listen carefully for the differences before you answer."

After these instructions were given, each child was asked the following sixteen questions:

1) *Specific/Unconditional*:

a) "Do you think that this person will hurt you again ?"

b) "Do you worry about being hurt by this person?"

c) "When you think about this person, do you feel like he or she will hurt you again?"

d) "Do you stay away from this person?"

2) *General/Unconditional*:

a) "Do you think that other people will hurt you?"

b) "Do you worry about being hurt by other people?"

c) "When you think about others, do you feel like they will hurt you?"

d) "Do you stay away from others?"

3) *Specific/Conditional*:

a) "Do you think that forgiving this person will cause a greater chance of your being hurt again by him or her?"

b) "Do you worry about being hurt by this person if you forgive them?"

c) "When you think about forgiving this person, do you feel like he or she will hurt you again?"

d) "If you forgive this person, will you have to stay away from them?"

4) *General/Conditional*:

a) "Do you think that forgiving this person will cause a greater chance of your being hurt by others?"

b) "Do you worry about being hurt by others if you forgive this person?"

c) "When you think about forgiving this person, do you feel like others will hurt you?"

d) "If you forgive this person, will you have to stay away from others?"

A 4-point Likert format page (yes, a little bit yes, a little bit no, no) was used to record participants' responses from a response board. The total score ranges from 64 (belief in strong likelihood of being hurt again) to 16 (belief in low likelihood of being hurt again). The scale provides scores ranging from 16 (strong likelihood) to 4 (low likelihood) for each of the 4 sub-scales. This allows for the means to separate an overall belief that one is vulnerable, from the belief that forgiving someone who hurt you deeply will leave you vulnerable to future hurt - both from the person who hurt you and from others. If a participant answered *yes* or a *little bit yes* to any part (a, b, c, d) of questions 3 and 4,), they were asked either or both of the following

questions corresponding to the Specific/Conditional (question 3), and to the General/Conditional

(question 4) subscales:

> 3) What do you think (worry, feel) it is about forgiving that would make him/her hurt you
> again?
>
> 4) Why would forgiving him/her cause others to hurt you?

Responses that included references to the offender's personalities and to the personalities of the

participants were of particular interest because these types of references support an entity view.

Procedure

All of the scales were administered orally by the experimenter, and in individual private

settings with each participant. Participants were given the Implicit Personality Theory

Questionnaire (Erdley & Dweck, 1993) to complete, after which they were interviewed

individually by the experimenter to complete the Enright Forgiveness Scale for Children (EFI-C;

Enright, 1993) and the Offense Expectation Scale for Children and Adolescents (OES-CA;

Beth). Response boards were used for all of the scales in order to aid the participants. Response

boards show the choice of answers visually and are generally used in studies with children.

Participants were instructed to answer orally. The response boards were provided only to assist

the participants in remembering the available response choices that were available. If the

participants answered *yes* or a *little bit yes* to either or both of the Conditional subscale questions

(Specific/Conditional, General/Conditional), they were asked either or both of the following

questions corresponding to the Specific/Conditional (question 3), and to the General/Conditional

(question 4) subscales:

3) What do you think (worry, feel) it is about forgiving that would make him(her) hurt you again?

4) Why would forgiving him(her) cause others to hurt you?

Responses were recorded by the experimenter for later analysis. Sessions conducted in the school samples were held during and after the regular school day at a non-intrusive time and area in the school. The sessions were pre-arranged with the Principal and the classroom teacher. Sessions conducted in the YMCA samples were held during free-time periods in after-school programs and in the YMCA day-camps.

Chapter 4: Method - Study 2

Participants

There were 54 adolescents participating in Study 2, all of whom were identified as entity

theorists in Study 1. The participants were randomly assigned in equal numbers to an

experimental (n=27) or control condition (n=27).

Materials and Procedure

The Implicit Personality Theory Questionnaire (Erdley and Dweck, 1993), the EFI-C

(Enright, 1993), and the OES-AC (Beth), described in Study 1, were also used in Study 2. In

addition, the Beck Anger Inventory for Youth (BANI-Y) was used to measure the entity

theorist's experience of anger. This inventory contains 20 statements about thoughts, feelings, or

behaviors associated with anger. Items include perceptions of mistreatment, negative thoughts

about others, feelings of anger, and physiological arousal. National norms, based on a stratified

standardization sample, are available as well as comparisons with scores obtained by a clinical

outpatient sample and a sample of children qualifying for special education. The inventory is

intended for use with children between the ages of 7 and 14. Responses for each item are

indicated by how frequently the statement is true for them. The items are written at the second

grade level for ease of understanding, but were administered orally by the experimenter to

individual participants in this study.

An intervention adapted from a study by Heyman and Dweck (1998) on children's beliefs

regarding socio-moral stability, was given to the experimental and the control groups by the

experimenter. Context-related causal explanation training (incremental theory) consisted of 3

scenarios depicting a hypothetical classmate behaving in what might be construed as an offending behavior. One version of each of the 3 scenarios has a male character, and the other a female character. This allows for the character's gender to be counterbalanced across participants. Participants were asked to think about why the character depicted in each scenario behaved in such a manner. The experimental group was reminded, before listening to each of the scenarios, that the questions in the scenarios were for them to think about only, and that they were not to answer the questions out loud. After a brief pause to allow time for the child to make his or her own judgment, the offending behavior was explained by the context in which it occurred, thus supporting an incremental view.

The scenarios and their accompanying context-related causal explanations are as follows: 1) Imagine a new girl in your class. She shouts bad names at you and trips you at recess. Why do you think she acted this way? (Brief pause)

Reframing: It turns out her classmates at the old school told her that the students at your school are very tough, and the only way to get anyone to like you was to act tough on the playground.

2) Imagine that your class is about to have a spelling contest and your teacher chooses two team captains, one each for the Red and Blue teams. Your best friend was selected to be the Red team captain, and because of the noise in the classroom there is some confusion concerning what your teacher means about the order. The Blue team captain begins to pick his friends to be on the Blue team. Your teacher stops the captains and calls them to his desk. After they return to their seats they proceed by selecting every other person for their teams. However, the first people chosen for each team remain on the team they were selected for. Why do you think your friend did not choose you for his team? (Brief pause)

Reframing: When your teacher called the two captains to his desk he explained that he wanted them to pick every other child in the order in which they were seated. He also said that those who already were picked for a team should stay on that team.

3) Imagine that you are eating lunch with your class when you see a girl putting some other people's unopened milk cartons into her backpack when they are not looking. You do not recognize the girl. Why do you think she is stealing the milk? (Brief pause)

Reframing: It turns out that the girl is homeless and a social worker bought her to school today. She is used to not having any milk, and was taking the cartons to share with her younger brothers.

The control group participants were also given the scenarios, but were asked to answer the questions themselves – therefore they were not given the context-related causal explanation that the experimental group heard. The responses given by the control group were recorded for analysis. Responses that included references to the story characters' personalities, and to the personalities of the control group participants were of interest because these types of references support an entity view.

Prior to the scenario presentations, the experimental and control groups were given the Beck Anger Inventory for Youth (BANI-Y) to complete. Then the experimenter presented the groups of entity theorists, randomly assigned to the experimental or control condition, with the 3 scenarios counterbalanced for gender. This presentation was conducted individually.

Immediately following the scenario presentations to individual participants in the two groups, all participants were again given the Implicit Personality Theory Questionnaire (Erdley & Dweck, 1993) and the Beck Anger Inventory for Youth (BANI-Y), and were re-interviewed with the EFI-C (Enright, 1993) and the OES-AC (Beth).

At pre-arranged times with school and YMCA officials (approximately 2 weeks later-between 13 & 15 days), there was a follow-up visit to the schools and the day camps. At this visit the experimental and control groups again completed the Implicit Personality Theory Questionnaire (Erdley and Dweck, 1993) and the Beck Anger Inventory for Youth (BANI-Y), and were re-interviewed with the EFI-C (Enright, 1993) and the OES-AC (Beth).

Chapter 5: Reliability of the Scales

This chapter summarizes the psychometric properties of the 3 scales used in Study 1 and

Study 2. The internal consistency of the inventories was assessed by Cronbach's alpha

coefficient, and by test-retest consistency of scores for the pre, post, and follow-up sessions

conducted in Study 2. Test-retest reliability coefficients are given in the correlation matrices. In

addition, the distribution of scores for the first administration of the Implicit Personality Theory

Questionnaire across theory type are provided by a bar graph in Figure 1. This distribution is of

interest because it provides the basis of the theory groupings for participants.

The Implicit Personality Theory Questionnaire (Erdley and Dweck, 1993)

Cronbach's alpha for the Implicit Personality Theory Questionnaire = .79. Means and

standard deviations and test-retest correlations are as follows.

Table 1 *Implicit Personality Theory Questionnaire: Means & Standard Deviations*

	Mean	Standard Deviation	N
Pre-test	1.7654	.36765	27
Post-test	1.6543	.32662	27
Follow-up	1.5802	.35316	27

Table 2 *Implicit Personality Theory Questionnaire: Test-retest Correlation Matrix*

	Pre-test	Post-test	Follow-up
Pre-test	1.000	.722	.496
Post-test	.722	1.000	.657
Follow-up	.496	.657	1.000

Figure 1 *Frequency of participants by scores on the Implicit Theory Questionnaire*

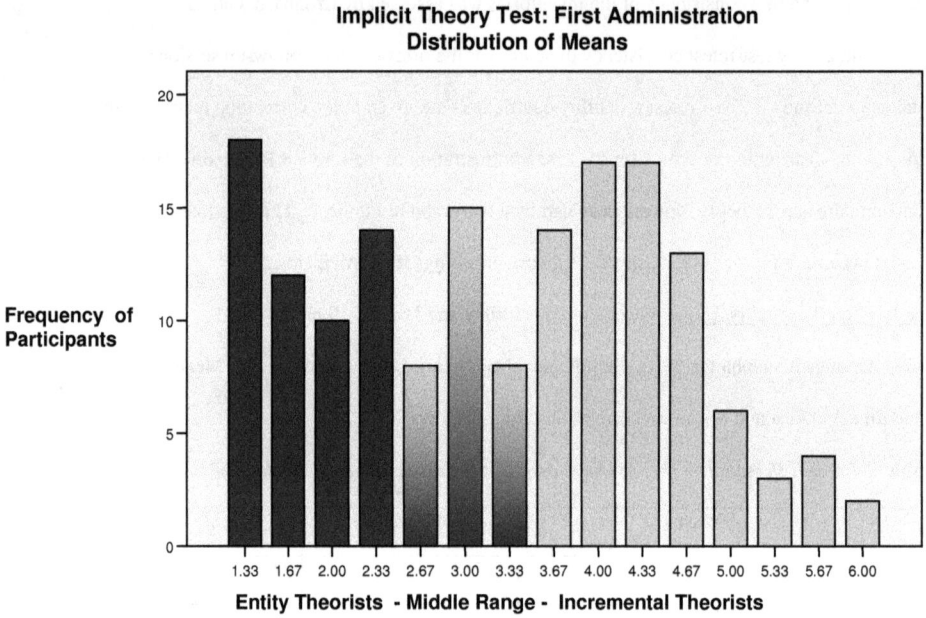

**Implicit Theory Test: First Administration
Distribution of Means**

Frequency of Participants

Entity Theorists - Middle Range - Incremental Theorists

The Enright Forgiveness Inventory for Children (Enright, 1993)

Cronbach's alpha for the Enright Forgiveness Inventory for Children = .93. Means and standard deviations and test-retest correlations are as follows.

Table 3 *Enright Forgiveness Inventory for Children: Means & Standard Deviations*

	Mean	Standard Deviation	N
Pre-test	76.9259	22.55579	27
Post-test	74.8889	25.40493	27
Follow-up	78.6667	27.02705	27

Table 4 *Enright Forgiveness Inventory for Children: Test-retest Correlation Matrix*

	Pre-test	Post-test	Follow-up
Pre-test	1.000	.974	.933
Post-test	.974	1.000	.883
Follow-up	.933	.883	1.000

Offense Expectation Scale for Children and Adolescents (Beth)

Cronbach's alpha for the Offense Expectation Scale for Children and Adolescents = .83. The inter-item correlation matrix supporting internal consistency is provided in the Appendix.

Table 5 *Offense Expectation Scale for Children and Adolescents: Means & Standard Deviations*

	Mean	Standard Deviation	N
Pre-test	25.7778	6.09750	27
Post-test	24.0741	8.42581	27

Follow-up	23.1852	7.04402	27

Table 6 *Offense Expectation Scale for Children and Adolescents: Test-rest Correlation Matrix*

	Pre-test	Post-test	Follow-up
Pre-test	1.000	.946	.825
Post-test	.946	1.000	.888
Follow-up	.825	.888	1.000

Chapter 6: Results - Study 1 Analyses

A two-tailed t-test was conducted with the overall scores from the first administration of the Enright Forgiveness Inventory for Children to determine which of the two groups of children, classified according to implicit theory, are the most forgiving. It was expected that those holding an incremental theory would be more forgiving. As predicted, this analysis yielded a significant mean difference between the two groups, showing the incremental theorists to be more forgiving, $t(2, 127) = -2.383$, $p = .019$. Participants holding an incremental theory scored higher ($M = 89.59$, $SD = 21.24$) than entity theorists who scored an average of 9 points lower ($M = 80.96$, $SD = 19.57$) at the initial testing.

A two-tailed t-test was conducted using the initial scores from the OES-AC to determine if the implicit theory groups differed in their overall expectation for future hurt. It was expected that participants holding an entity theory's expectations for future hurt would be higher than those holding an incremental theory. However, the analysis did not yield a significant mean difference between the two groups, $t(2, 127 = 1.755, p = .082)$.

It was expected that those holding an entity theory would have higher expectations for future hurt from the *specific* person that hurt them deeply, than would the incremental theorists. A two-tailed t-test was conducted on the combined subscales (Specific/unconditional and Specific/conditional). Analysis did not yield a significant difference between the groups, $t(2, 127 = 1.126, p = .262)$. However, a two-tailed t-test of the scores on Specific/conditional scale *alone* did come close to a significant mean difference between the two groups, $t(2, 127) = 1.938$, $p = .055$). Although not statistically significant, the means suggest that entity theorists ($M = 8.59$, $SD = 3.39$) expected to be hurt by the specific person that hurt them previously - if they were to forgive that individual - to a greater degree than did the incremental theorists ($M = 7.45$,

SD = 3.23).

It was also expected that feelings of *overall* vulnerability would be higher for entity theorists if they were asked to forgive the individual who hurt them deeply. This was not the case. A two-tailed t-test of the General/Conditional subscale scores did not yield a significant difference between the means of the two groups, $t(2, 127) = .974$, $p = .332$.

Of interest were the participants responses to the following questions corresponding to the Specific/Conditional (question 3), and to the General/Conditional (question 4) subscales of the Offense Expectation Scale foe Children and Adolescents (OES-CA; Beth) if they answered *yes* or a *little bit yes* to any of the Conditional subscale questions:

> 3) What do you think (worry, feel) it is about forgiving that would make him/her hurt you again?
>
> 4) Why would forgiving him/her cause others to hurt you?

The recorded responses given by the participants were coded for references to personality (self & other), references to condoning the offending behavior (i.e. "I'd be like – saying it was OK to do that."), and for references to *re*-angering the offender (i.e. "Talking to him would irritate him. He doesn't care what you say."). Responses that included references to the offender's personalities and to the personalities of the participants were of particular interest because these types of references support an entity view. Condoning responses, and *re*-angering responses are of interest because they may be indicative of a fear of being hurt again by the offender. Transcripts were coded by the experimenter and an independent rater to insure reliability. Scores were calculated by dividing the frequency of codes identified by each rater by the sum of the total possible codes in each transcript and compared point-to point. There was an overall 100% point-to-point agreement on items coded for.

Table 7 shows the references to the personalities of the offender and to self according to the participants' implicit theory. The highest frequency of references were to being viewed as weak. Table 2 shows references to condoning the offending behavior (i.e. "I'd be like – saying it was OK to do that."), and Table 3 shows references to *re*-angering the offender (i.e. "Talking to him would irritate him. He doesn't care what you say.").

Table 7 *References To Personality - Offender and Self By Implicit Theory In Response To Questions 3 & 4.*

Implicit theory:	Mid		Incrementa l		Entity	
Total participants :	32		75		54	
Yes and *a little bit yes* responses:	19		25		30	
	Self	Other	Self	Other	Self	Other
Personality references:	3	2	9	2	12	2
References to *weak*	2	0	8	0	6	0
References to *dumb*	0	0	0	0	4	0

Table 8 *References To Condoning By Implicit Theory In Response To Questions 3 & 4.*

Implicit	Mid	Incremental	Entity

theory:			
Total participants:	32	75	54
Yes and *a little bit yes* responses:	19	25	30
Condoning references	7	5	2

Table 9 *References To Re-Angering The Offender By Implicit Theory In Response To Questions 3 & 4.*

Implicit theory:	Mid	Incremental	Entity
Total participants:	32	75	54
Yes and *a little bit yes* responses:	19	25	30
Re angering references	1	3	6

Chapter 7: Results - Study 2 Analyses

It was expected that the experimental group scores for both the immediate and follow-up post-tests would reflect an increase in forgiveness and a decrease in expectations to be hurt again. A 2 x 3 (experimental/control group x sessions: pre, post, & follow-up) analysis of variance was conducted to analyze the scores of the EFI-C (Enright, 1993), and a 2 x 3 (experimental/control group x sessions: pre, post, & follow-up) analysis of variance was conducted on the overall scores from the OES-CA (Beth). As expected, there was a significant interaction in favor of the intervention demonstrated by an increase in forgiveness for the experimental group at the immediate post-test $F(1,53) = 4.119, p = .048$, and a significant interaction in favor of the intervention demonstrated by an increase in forgiveness for the experimental group at the follow-up post-test $F(1, 53) = 5.375, p = .024$. Contrary to prediction, the greatest increase in forgiveness scores for the experimental group was found at the follow-up post test (+ 8 points post and + 2.5 points immediate), and not at the immediate post-test. There was a significant interaction in favor of the intervention demonstrated by a decrease in overall expectations to be hurt again (- 3 points) for the experimental group at the follow-up post-test $F(1, 53) = 4.860, p = .032$, but although in the right direction, not at the immediate post-test $F(1, 53) = 3.470, p = .068$.

Correlational analysis was conducted on the scores from the Implicit Personality theory Questionnaire (Erdley & Dweck, 1993) and the forgiveness (EFI-C; Enright, 1993) scores for both the immediate and follow-up post-tests. It was expected that there would be a positive relationship between the scores on the Implicit Personality Theory Questionnaire and the scores on the EFI-C. As expected, there was a significant positive correlation for both the immediate $r(52) = .35, p = .005$, and for the follow-up post tests $r(52) = .33, p = .009$. As a shift toward an incremental view occurred, so did an increase in the propensity to forgive.

In addition, correlational analysis was conducted with the scores from the Implicit

Personality Theory Questionnaire and the vulnerability scores from the Specific/conditional sub-

scale of the OES-AC (Beth) for both of the post-tests. It was expected that those showing the

least shift in perspective toward an incremental view will also feel the most vulnerable to future

hurt from one who has deeply hurt them in the past, if they are asked to forgive that individual.

Although the scales were negatively correlated for both the immediate and follow-up post-tests,

the correlations were not statistically significant, immediate post-test: $r(52) = -.271$, $p =$

$.086(52)$, follow-up post-test: $r = -.225$, $p = .129$.

A 2 x 3 (experimental/control group x sessions: pre, post, & follow-up) analysis of

variance was used to analyze the pre- and post-intervention scores from the Beck Anger

Inventory for Youth (BANI-Y). It was expected that entity theorists who received training in

context-related causal explanation for behavior (experimental condition) would show a greater

reduction in general feelings of anger than the entity theorists in the control condition would.

However, the reduction of anger was not significant for either group at the immediate post-test:

$F(1, 53) = 1.556$, $p = .218$; nor at the follow-up post-test: $F(1, 53) = .353$, $p = .555$.

The recorded responses given by the control group were coded for references to

personality (self & other). References to personality were coded with a number 1 and references

and all other responses were coded as 0. Of the personality references, self references were

coded as S, and references to others were coded as O. Responses that included references to the

story characters' personalities and to the personalities of the control group participants were of

interest because these types of references support an entity view. Transcripts were coded by the

experimenter and an independent rater to insure reliability. Scores were calculated by dividing

the frequency of codes identified by each rater by the sum of the total possible codes in each transcript and compared point-to point. There was an overall 100% point-to-point agreement

on items coded. Out of 81 total responses (3 per each of the 27 control group participants), 36

contained references to personality. Of the 36 references, 24 were to other, and 12 were to self.

All references were to negative personality traits (i.e. dumb, mean, bully). Table 4 shows the

responses broken down by question. The three questions are given here again for easy reference:

1) Why do you think she acted this way?

2) Why do you think your best friend did not choose you for his team?

3) Why do you think she is stealing the milk?

Table 10 *Control Group Responses From The Context-Related Causal Explanation Stories*

Story responses:	Self	Other
Question 1	2/27	14/27
Question 2	10/27	0/27
Question 3	0/27	10/27

Chapter 8: Discussion

The main focus of these studies was to find ways to help children to be more forgiving of others even when they have suffered a deep personal hurt by a peer. We know that feelings of anger and revenge caused by deep hurt can be dissuaded through forgiveness (Enright & Fitzgibbons, 2000). Central to the purpose of helping children to forgive is to identify psychological dimensions, such as attributions for behavior that may help or hinder forgiving someone that caused the hurt.

Study 1

There were four hypotheses for Study 1 and two of those were supported. The significant findings, that incremental theorists are more forgiving than entity theorists and have less expectations for future hurt, set the stage for future research and understanding in how attributions for behavior affect forgiveness. Study 1 shows that those holding an incremental theory of attribution are more forgiving than those holding an entity view. There can be several reasons for this, one of them being that entity theorists tend to label others, a practice that tends to dehumanize individuals categorizing them as the "out" group. Entity theorist believe that these "out" group members have nothing in common with them, do not like the same toys or games, do not have the usual needs and preferences, or worries and concerns. The "out" group is labeled as a separate (and inferior) class of children – one in which they do not want to interact with (Levy & Dweck, 1999). Therefore, there seems little point to forgiving someone from the "out" group. Many children and adults believe erroneously that forgiveness means that you are demonstrating to the offender a desire for reconciliation (Enright & Fitzgibbons, 2000). Why reconcile with someone with whom you do not want a relationship?

It is important that we understand and teach children and adolescents that forgiveness and reconciliation are distinct processes. Forgiveness is a free choice to abandon resentment and adopt a more positive outlook toward an offender. Because of this, forgiveness can be unconditional. Reconciliation, on the other hand, can and most often should be conditioned on the offender's willingness and ability to change the offensive ways. The concern of many of the participants in this study was worrying about being viewed as weak or dumb by the offender and by other peers. This concern suggests that these young adolescents believed that forgiveness involves going to the offender and verbally forgiving face to face. This belief acts as a stumbling block to forgiveness by preventing the offender from realizing the positive psychological and emotional self-benefits of forgiveness. Children and adolescents should be taught that forgiving someone does not mean that you have to necessarily go and tell them that they are forgiven. Reconciliation is separate and need not occur in conjunction with forgiveness.

In addition, the act of dehumanizing one who has hurt you can have a debilitating effect on the ability to forgive that individual. The understanding that another possesses unconditional worth plays a key role in the forgiveness process (Enright & the Human Development Study Group, 1991). The forgiver sees that no matter what another does, he or she is still worthy of respect and empathy because of personhood. It is difficult to have empathy for another if you do not believe that they share the common experience of humanity with you.

Another, more disturbing reason that entity theorists are less willing to forgive may be because they believe that bad people should be punished or harmed (Chin, Dweck, Tong, & Fu, 1997). In this set of studies by Chin et al. (1997), participants were asked to assume the role of a teacher dealing with children who had not completed their classroom assignments. Entity theorists were more likely to mete out punishment, whereas incremental theorists suggested mutual negotiation – asking the children why they were have difficulty and discussing remedies for the situation. In the present study, incremental theorists were far more willing to forgive those who had hurt them deeply. This willingness suggests that trying to change children's implicit theories toward an incremental view may have a strong influence on their willingness to forgive.

It was also expected that entity theorists would be more fearful of future hurt, specifically from the peer who had hurt them deeply. Although by a simple comparison of the means, entity theorist felt more concerned with future hurt than incremental theorists when conditioned upon forgiving this person, the statistical analysis did not yield significant results. However, a p value of .055 suggests some support for this hypothesis. Taken together with the qualitative responses given by participants asking them why they were fearful of future hurt, there is unarguably a psychological variable here that needs closer inspection. Therefore, the participants answers to the following questions corresponding to the Specific/Conditional (question 3), and to the General/Conditional (question 4) subscales of the Offense Expectation Scale foe Children and Adolescents (OES-CA; Beth) are of particular interest:

3) What do you think (worry, feel) it is about forgiving that would make him (her) hurt you again?

4) Why would forgiving him (her) cause others to hurt you?

As expected, the highest frequency of references to personality traits were made by entity theorists, however the references were not to the personality traits of the offender. These references were made to self-characteristics – being viewed as *weak* (6 out of 12) or *dumb* (4 out of 12). Interestingly, incremental theorists (8 out of 9) and participants who fell in the Mid-range (2 out of 3) on theory preference were also concerned with being viewed as weak. It is likely that the definition of weak varies among children by theory – entity theorists likely see the characteristic as a more stable trait label, while incremental theorists view being weak as a behavior. Future research into variances in beliefs about the definitions of personality traits may sort this out. All of the past implicit theory research suggests this to be true (Dweck & Ehrlinger, 2005). In any case, being thought of as weak was a major concern to all of the children in this study. It is likely that we are implicitly teaching our children that to forgive is a sign of weakness, and the appearance of strength is a more desirable stance to take in any conflict situation. This is a tendency that should be addressed in our schools and communities. The opposite appears to be true – forgiveness often takes more strength – especially for an entity theorist who believes that forgiving will effect little change on the offender, missing the self-benefits that can be gained through forgiveness.

Entity theorists were also more concerned with re-angering the offender by forgiving them. This is a belief that is congruent with believing that someone holds a stable personality and is unlikely to change. Mid-range and incremental theorists were more concerned than entity theorists that forgiving the offender would be a sign of condoning their behavior. This belief, focused on behavior, is consistent with an incremental view. To date, we know little about the beliefs of children who fall into the Mid-range on implicit theories. Research including or focused on the Mid-range group is needed so that we do not make the mistake of overlooking these young people.

Study 2

As in Study 1, only half of the six hypotheses proved true in Study 2. However, once again, the important hypotheses did prove to be true. It was expected that the experimental group's scores of both the immediate and follow-up post-tests would reflect an increase in forgiveness and a decrease in expectations to be hurt again. As in other intervention studies designed to change the implicit theories of individuals (Heslin, Lathan, and VandeWalle, 2005; Nussaum and Dweck, 2005; Blackwell, Trzesniewski, & Dweck, 2005; Good, Aronson, & Inzlicht, 2003; Aronson, Fried, & Good, 2002; Levy & Dweck, 1999; Levy, Stroessner, & Dweck, 1998), there was a significant interaction in favor of the intervention demonstrated by an increase in forgiveness for the experimental group at the immediate post-test and at the follow-up post-test, and a decrease in the concern for future hurt at the follow-up post test.

This study's aim was to learn if young adolescents would become more forgiving and less worried about future hurt, as their implicit theories changed. Therefore, correlational analyses were also conducted. As a shift toward an incremental view occurred, so did an increase in the propensity to forgive. A shift toward the incremental view was negatively associated with a decline in worry about future hurt. Although not statistically significant; this tendency might be found in a larger sample – or with more training. This study demonstrates that tendencies toward hatred and revenge can be changed through interventions focused on drawing attention to the situations in which deep hurt occurs. Since greater gains were seen at the follow-up session, there appears to be an effect of time, perhaps time to "mull things over" and to reconsider the events surrounding one's own specific deep hurt. Therefore, teachers and educators should not be discouraged if they do not see immediate effects of implicit theory training, but should continue to illustrate to their students how all human actions are affected by situational factors.

It appears that changing an individual's implicit theory does not automatically erase feelings of anger. Anger is a deep and often abiding emotion. Enright and colleagues (Enright & Fitzgibbons, 2000) have had success at reducing anger in individuals who have been deeply hurt. It is this author's recommendation that forgiveness interventions designed by Enright et al. (1994) be combined with implicit theory interventions for optimal change and benefit to those who have been deeply hurt. However, teaching children and adults that human behavior is influenced and often dictated by surrounding events is likely to have a profound a-priori effect on an individual's coping with deep hurt through the means of forgiveness, empathy, and understanding, rather than anger and revenge. Longitudinal research is needed to learn how frequent, and to what degree, implicit theory training may be effective at reducing feelings of anger and revenge throughout development and across the life-span.

Responses that included references to the story characters' personalities and to the personalities of the control group participants were of interest because stable-trait references support an entity view. These three questions were asked of all of the entity theorists after the intervention stories were given, however, recall that the experimental group was instructed not to answer. They were given implicit theory training. The control group did not receive the implicit theory training, but were instead instructed to answer the following questions.

1) Why do you think she acted this way?

2) Why do you think your best friend did not choose you for his team?

3) Why do you think she is stealing the milk?

The control group (n = 27) gave a total of 3 responses each to the story questions, out of which 36 of those responses were to personality traits. Therefore, a little less than half of the reasons given for the story characters' behavior supported an entity view. Consistent with the question, all of the stable-trait references were to self for Question 2. These participants felt

that their friends did not choose them because they were *dumb,* and therefore were bad spellers.

They seemed to ignore the information about the teacher calling the team captains to her desk for

further team selection instructions. Most or all of the references to personality traits given were

to others in response to Question 1 and Question 3. These references were made to the story

character being *mean* or being a *bully.* These were the reasons given for why a peer pushed you

at recess (14 out of 27), and why a child stole milk from others at lunch time (10 out of 27).

Question 2 may be the most interesting because it gives speculative information that

many children appeared to miss or ignore. Other studies found that entity theorists are willing to

label others as good or bad, or as moral or immoral, on the basis of little evidence (Erdley &

Dweck, 1993: Chiu et al., 1997). This study demonstrates that even though contrary information

was given, it was disregarded by almost all of the control group when making a judgment about

their best friend's behavior. This is a challenging finding given that judgments such as "My

friend was just being mean" or, "She's a bully" can lead to anger and revenge. not

understanding and forgiveness.

Limitations

There are some limitations to these studies, one of them being the introduction of a new

scale. However, we now have gathered information regarding the reasons why young

adolescents who feel they will be hurt again if they forgive, feel the way they do. Future

validation studies of the scale can include questions that directly assess concerns about being

viewed as weak, and about condoning offenses.

There are also limits in drawing a sample of participants from a mid-sized, Mid-Western college town. There is evidence in the literature that cross-cultural differences in implicit

theories exist, therefore, it is important to examine how these differences are related to

forgiveness. Those growing up in Eastern cultures generally attribute a behavior to the situation

in which the behavior occurred (Rosati, Knowles, Kalish, Gopnik, Ames, & Morris, 2001;

Morris & Peng, 1994). Some attention has been given to ethnic and socio-economic differences.

The participants in Levy and Dweck's (1999) Study 1 were primarily Latino/ Hispanic

American (71.8%), and from a large public school in New York City. The participants for their

Study 2 were also from a New York school, but were ethnically diverse: 27.3% African

American, 2.3% Asian American, 34.1% European American, 36.3% Latino/ Hispanic

American. These and other studies regarding how culture influences what types of attributions

we make, strongly suggests that implicit theories are shaped more by culture and not by ethnicity

or socio-economic status (Rosati, Knowles, Kalish, Gopnik, Ames, & Morris, 2001; Morris &

Peng, 1994).

Conclusions

There are benefits of including implicit theory training in schools, as well as the obvious

benefits to the work of school psychologists and other clinicians. As previously stated in the

introduction, when individuals continually tend to overestimate the danger of potentially

stressful situations, anxiety disorders begin to develop (Bogels & Zigterman, 2000). Inward-

focused negative emotions, such as self-blame and guilt, are activated when individuals hold

themselves responsible for negative outcomes, blaming the other party is associated with

negative outward emotions such as anger and hostility (Tangney & Dearing, 2002). In addition,

a belief that negative personality traits are stable and unchangeable may contribute to a host of social interaction difficulties throughout the life-span.

Implicit theories create powerful frameworks through which we understand and interpret our world. Our judgments for self and others and our behaviors are based on these interpretations. Dweck (2005) has identified three main areas in which implicit theories play a role in conflict resolution:

1) The rapidity and rigidity with which people label others as well as the ways in which these labels distance and dehumanize others.

2) The conflict resolutions people use (revenge versus understanding).

3) The willingness to reveal deficiencies and admit fault to solve problems and learn.

The present studies have demonstrated that the willingness of young adolescents to forgive a peer who has hurt them deeply, can be increased by teaching an incremental theory of attribution through short stories whose contexts are relevant to young people. The fear of being hurt again in the future was also reduced, a fear that may hinder the willingness to forgive. Although the association between the implicit theory shift and worries about being hurt by the specific offending peer if one where to forgive him or her was not significant, it is likely that greater benefits would be realized through a more extensive training program. In addition, correlational analyses are sensitive to sample size. The small number of participants in the experimental group (n = 27) may have influenced the results.

Research has shown that people who forgive can decrease anger, anxiety, and depression (Enright & Fitzgibbons, 2000). Studies conducted by Enright and his colleagues demonstrate that forgiveness is linked to healthy emotional regulation. This study lends some insight into how an individual's implicit theory and the accompanying attributions can affect a willingness to forgive. More importantly, this study demonstrates that an individual's implicit theory can be changed, thereby increasing the willingness to forgive.

Programs of future research designed to explore how implicit theories are associated with various relationships and related to psychological processes, such as forgiveness, are potentially rich venues for understanding the development of implicit theories and for interventions designed to promote psychological well-being in children and adults. This study replicates the findings of Levy and Dweck (1998), showing when theories about the malleability of traits are temporarilyinduced, individuals show similar patterns to those with pre-existing theories. Better understanding how biases and fears form and develop, will better equip researchers, clinicians, and teachers to offer help and instruction on how to avoid misunderstandings, labeling, and discord with one another through forgiveness.

References

Abrahamson, L. Y., Seligman, M. E., & Teasdale, J. D. (1978). Learned helplessness in humans: Critique and reformulation. Journal of Abnormal Psychology, 87, 49-74.

Al-Mabuk, R., Enright, R. D., & Cardis, P. (1995). Forgiveness education with parentally love-deprived college students. Journal of Moral Education, 24, 427-444.

Aronson, J., Fried, C., & Good, C. (2002). Reducing the effects of stereotype threat on African American college students by shaping theories of intelligence. Journal of Experimental Social Psychology, 38, 113-125.

Austin, S., & Joseph, S. (1996). Assessment of bully/victim problems in 8- to 11-year-olds. British Journal of Education and Psychology, 66, 447-456.

Bagels, S. M. & Zigterman, D. (2000). Dysfunctional cognitions in children with social phobia, separation anxiety disorder, and generalized anxiety disorder. Journal of Abnormal Child Psychology, 28, 205-211.

Barenboim, C. (1981). The development of person perception in childhood and adolescence: From behavioral comparisons to psychological constructs to psychological comparisons. Child Development, 52(1), 129-144.

Blackwell, L. S., Trzesniewski, K., & Dweck, C. S. (2003). Implicit theories of intelligence predict achievement across an adolescent transition: A longitudinal study and an intervention. Submitted for publication.

Boulton, M. J. (1997). Teachers' views on bullying: Definitions, attitudes and ability to cope. British Journal of Education and Psychology, 67, 223-233.

Boulton, M. J., & Underwood, K. (1992). Bully/victim problems among middle school children. British Journal of Education and Psychology, 62, 73-87.

Brown, R., & Hewsstone, M. (2005). An integrative theory of intergroup conflict. Advances in Experimental Social Psychology, 37, 255-343.

Cheng, P., & Nowick, L. (1992). Covariation in natural causal induction. Psychological Review, 99, 365-382.

Chiu, C. (1994). Bases of categorization and person cognition. Unpublished doctoral dissertation, Columbia University.

Chiu, C., Dweck, C. S., Tong, Y. Y., & Fu, J. H. (1997). Implicit theories and conceptions of morality. Journal of Personality and Social Psychology, 73, 923-940.

Chiu, C., Hong, H., & Dweck, C. S. (1997). Lay dispositionism and implicit theories of personality. Journal of Personality and Social Psychology, 73, 19-30.

Coyle, C. T., & Enright, R. D. (1997). Forgiveness intervention with post-abortion men. Journal of Consulting and Clinical Psychology, 65, 1042-1046.

Dweck, C. S. & Ehlinger, J. (2005). In M. Deutsch, P. Coleman, & E. Marcus (Eds.) The Handbook of Conflict Resolution, Vol. 2. San Francisco: Jossey-Bass.

Dweck, C. S., & Leggett, E. L. (1988). A social-cognitive approach to motivation and personality. Psychological Review, 95, 256-273.

Dweck, C. S., Chiu, C., & Hong, Y. (1995). Implicit theories and their role in judgments and reactions: A world from two perspectives. Psychological Inquiry, 6, 267-285.

Enright, R. D. (1994). The Enright Forgiveness Inventory. (Available from the International Forgiveness Institute, P.O. Box Madison, WI 53716 or at www. Forgiveness Insitute.org).

Enright, R. D., & Fitzgibbons, R. P. (2000). Helping Clients Forgive: An Empirical Guide for Resolving Anger and Restoring Hope. Washington, DC: American Psychological Association.

Enright, R. D., & North, J. (Eds.). (!998). Exploring Forgiveness. Madison: University of Wisconsin Press.

Enright, R. D., and the Human Development Study Group (1991). The moral development of forgiveness. In W. Kurtines & J. Gewirtz (Eds.), Handbook of Moral Behavior and Development. (Vol. 1, pp. 123-152). Hillsdale, NJ: Erlbaum.

Enright, R. D., and the Human Development Study Group (1994). Piaget on the moral development of forgiveness: Reciprocity or identity? Human Development, 37, 63-80.

Erdley, C. A., & Dweck, C. S., (1993). Children's implicit personality theories as predictors of their social judgements. Child Development, 64, 863-878.

Erdley, C. A., Dweck, C. S., Loomis, C. C., Cain, K. M., & Dumas-Hines, F., (1997). Relations among children's social goals, implicit personality theories, and responses to social failure. Developmental Psychology, 33 (2), 263-272.

Federal Bureau of Investigation. (1998). Crime in the United States: Uniform Crime Reports. Washington, DC: U.S. Department of Justice.

Fitzgibbons, R. P. (1986). The cognitive and emotional uses of forgiveness in the treatment of anger. Psychotherapy, 23, 629-633.

Fitzgibbons, R. P. (1998). Anger and the healing power of forgiveness: A psychiatrist's view. In R. Enright & J. North (Eds.), Exploring Forgiveness (pp.63-74). Madison: University of Wisconsin Press.

Flavell, J. (1985). Cognitive Development. Hillsdale, NJ: Erlbaum.

Fombonne, E. (1998). Suicidal behaviors in vulnerable adolescents: Time and their correlates. British Journal of Psychiatry, 173, 154-159.

Freedman, S. R., & Enright, R. D. (1996). Forgiveness as an intervention goal with incest survivors. Journal of Consulting and Clinical Psychology, 64, 983-992.

Gable, S. & Peterson, L. (1998). School-aged children's attributions about their own naturally occurring minor injuries: A process analysis. Journal of Pediatric Psychology, 23, 323-332.

Gambaro, 2002. Unpublished doctoral dissertation, University of Wisconsin - Madison.

Gellman, S. A., Coley, J. D., & Gottfried, G. M. (1994). Essentialist beliefs in children: The acquisition of concepts and theories. In L. Hirschfeld and S. A. Gelman (Eds.), Mapping the Mind: Domain Specificity in Cognition and Culture. New York: Cambridge University Press

Good, C., Aronson, J., & Inzlicht, M. (2003). Improving adolescents standardized test performance: An intervention to reduce the effects of stereotype threat. Journal of Applied Developmental Psychology, 24, 645-662.

Hanan, H. & Power, T. G. (2004). Children's appraisal of major life events. American Journal of Orthopsychiatry, 74(1), 26-32.

Hebl, J. H. & Enright, R. D. (1993). Forgiveness as a psychotherapeutic goal with elderly females. Psychotherapy, 30, 658-667.

Heider, F. (1958). The Psychology of Interpersonal Relations. New York: Wiley

Hepp-Dax, S. H. (1996). Forgiveness as an educational goal with fifth-grade inner-city children. Unpublished doctoral dissertation, Fordham University, New York.

Heslin, P. A., Lathan G. P., & VandeWalle, D. (2005). The effect of implicit person theory on performance appraisals. Journal of Applied Psychology, 90, 842-856.

Heyman, G. D., & Dweck, C. S. (1998). Children's thinking about traits: Implications for judgements of the self and others. Child Development, 64 (2), 391- 403.

Holmgren, M. R. (1993, October). Forgiveness and the intrinsic value of persons. American Philosophical Quarterly, 30, 341-352.

Holmgren, M. R. (1997, April/May). Forgiveness and self-respect. World of Forgiveness, 1(2), 5-8.

Hong, Y. (1994). Predicting trait versus process inferences: The role of implicit theories. Unpublished doctoral dissertation, Columbia: New York.

Hope, D. (1987), The healing paradox of forgiveness. Psychotherapy, 24, 240-244.

Ichheiser, (1970). Social perception and moral judgment. Philosophy and Phenomenological Research, 26 (4), 546-560.

Juvonen, J., Graham, S., & Schuster, M. A (2003). Bullying among young adolescents: The strong, the weak, and the troubled. Pediatrics, 112(6), 1231-1237.

Kelley, H. (1967). Attribution theory in social psychology. In D. Levine (Ed.), Nebraska Symposium on Motivation. Lincoln: University of Nebraska Press.

Lazarus, R. S. (1991). Emotion and Adaptation. New York: Oxford University Press.

Levy, S. R, & Dweck, C. S. (1998). Trait- versus process-focused social judgement. Social Cognition, 16, 151-172.

Levy, S. R, & Dweck, C. S. (1999). The impact of children's static versus dynamic conceptions of people on stereotype formation. Child Development, 70 (5), 1163-1180.

Levy, S. R., Stroessner, S. J., & Dweck, C. S. (1998). Stereotype formation and endorsement: The role of implicit theories. Journal of Personality and Social Psychology, 74, 1421 - 1436.

Livesley, W., & Bromley, B. (1973). Person Perception in Childhood and Adolescence. New York: Wiley

Nolen-Hoeksena, S., Girgus, J. S., & Seligman, M. E. (1992). Predictions and consequences of childhood depressive symptoms: A 5-year longitudinal study. Journal of Abnormal Psychology, 101, 405-422.

North, J. (1987). Wrongdoing and forgiveness. Philosophy (62), 499-508.

Nussbaum, D. & Dweck, C. S. (2005). Self theories and modes of self-esteem maintenance. Unpublished data: Stanford University.

Park, Y. O. (1989). The development of forgiveness in the context of friendship conflict. Unpublished doctoral dissertation, University of Wisconsin-Madison.

Peng, K., & Nisbett, R. (2002). Cross-cultural similarities and differences in the understanding of physical causality. University of California.

Piaget, J. (1926). The Language and Thought of the Child. New York: Harcourt Brace

Piaget, J. (1955). Motivity, perception and intelligence. Enfance, 9 (2), 9-14.

Plaks, J., & Dweck, C. S. (1997, May). Implicit person theories and attention to counter-expectant social information. Paper presented at the Eighth Annual Convention of the American

Psychological Society, Washington, DC.

Rand Corporation (2005). Bullying in schools: Pervasive, disruptive, and serious. Center for Adolescent Health Promotion: Los Angeles. www.rand.org/health/adolescent.html

Rogoff, B., & Mistry, J. (1990). The social and functional context of children's remembering. In R. Fivush & J. Hudson (Eds.), Knowing and Remembering in Young Children. Cambridge, New York: Cambridge University Press.

Rosati, A., Knowles, E., Kalish, C., Gopnik, A. Ames, D., & Morris, M. (2001). The rocky road from acts to dispositions: Insights for attribution theory from developmental research on theories of mind. In B. Malle, L. Moses, & D. Baldwin (Eds.), Intentions and intentionality: Foundations of social cognition. Cambridge, MA: MIT Press.

Seligman, M. E. (1975). Helplessness: On Depression, Development, and Death. San Francisco, CA: Freeman.

Shatz, M., Wellman, H., & Silber, S. (1983). The acquisition of mental verbs: A systematic investigation of the first reference to mental state. Cognition, 14, 301-321.

Snyder, J. (1994). National Report on Juvenile Offending and Victimization. Washington, DC: American Psychiatric Press.

Sorich, L., & Dweck, C. S. (1996). Implicit theories as predictors of attributions for and response to wrong-doing. Unpublished raw data, Columbia University.

Subkoviak, M. J., Enright, R. D., Wu, C., Gassin, E., Freedman, S., Olson, L., & Sarinopoulos, I. (1992, April). Measuring interpersonal forgiveness. Paper presented at the annual meeting for the American Educational Research Association, San Francisco.

Subkoviak, M. J., Enright, R. D., Wu, C., Gassin, E., Freedman, S., Olson, L., & Sarinopoulos, I (1995). Measuring interpersonal forgiveness in late adolescence and middle adulthood. Journal of Adolescence 18, 641-655.

Tangney, J. P. & Dearing, R. L. (2002). Shame and Guilt. New York: Guilford Press. The Federal Interagency Forum on Child and Family Statistics (2003). America's Children: Key National Indicators of Well-Being http://www.childstats.gov/americaschildren/index.asp

Wellman, H. (1990). The Child's Theory of Mind. Cambridge, MA: MIT Press

Yuill, N. (1992). Children's conception of personality traits. Human Development, 35, 265-279.

Yuill, N., & Pearson, A. (1998). The development of bases for trait attribution: Children's understanding of traits as causal mechanisms for desires. Developmental Psychology, 34, 574-506.

www.ingramcontent.com/pod-product-compliance
Lightning Source LLC
Chambersburg PA
CBHW072156020426
42334CB00018B/2033